MotoJitsu
Master Riding Program Volume 2

Greg Widmar

Copyright © Greg Widmar
All rights reserved.
First Edition, 2020.

No part of this publication may be reproduced
without prior written permission from the Publisher.

Published by:
MotoJitsu, LLC
San Diego, CA 92169

ISBN: 979-8-670-91189-4

www.motojitsu.com

Special thanks

to all my MotoJitsu supporters around the world and to Andy at Immortal Concepts Studios for the amazing front and back cover images.

Materials needed

Sidewalk chalk
Clean parking lot
Tape measure 30 ft or longer
Small cones or tennis balls cut in half
(https://leeparksdesign.com/cones/)

MotoJitsu drills are not meant to replace any formal motorcycle course you may take. Rather, they are a structured set of drills you can practice between courses to enhance your motorcycle knowledge and riding ability.

I highly recommend warming up your tires prior to any higher speed drills. You can do this by weaving back and forth at around 20 mph in a straight line and/or hard acceleration and braking in a straight line.

Additionally, be aware of the grip your tires have in the area you're practicing. Slurry coat, painted lines, colder temperatures, broken pavement, or grass growing in cracks are all conditions that can lower your traction. Practice at your own risk.

The drills outlined in this book, performed incorrectly, could result in serious injury or death. The author encourages attending numerous motorcycle courses and wearing full, quality gear before attempting any of the drills. The author/publisher disclaims any liability incurred in connection with the use of the concepts outlined in this book. Whether practicing on public roads, at a racetrack, or at the local parking lot, you are responsible for your own safety.

Contents

Materials needed	v
Foreword	1
Preface	3
Snowman	4
3 3s	8
Eyeballs	12
Don't Die	16
Corner Speed	20
Crazy 13	24
Conversion to Metric	28
What's the Point?	29

Foreword by Dave Bianco

When Greg first started coming to the motorcycle training center on Marine Corps Base Camp Pendleton in 2013, he would regularly ask me to work with him one-on-one. During these training sessions, we would go over different skills as well as the basic knowledge needed for safe riding. Greg was still active duty back then, so I suggested he take some of the other classes offered on base, like the Total Control Intermediate Riding Clinic (IRC) and the Total Control Advanced Riding Clinics (ARC) Levels 1 and 2, as well as practicing on the lot next to our building.

In 2015, the state of California switched its basic program over to the Total Control Beginner Riding Clinic, aka the California Motorcyclist Safety Program Motorcyclist Training Course (CMSP MTC). Greg was on a very short list of people I wanted to get into the initial certification, as his drive to continuously improve is contagious and he was already involved with motorcycle education. Greg's passion for progress as a rider led me to encourage him to become an IRC and ARC instructor, as well a trainer for the CMSP MTC.

Greg's dedication to practice and desire to improve his knowledge and skill with motorcycles is so impressive we often switch roles. I now work with him doing his MotoJitsu drills to help improve my skills too, so Greg is now both a mentor and a student to me. I count Greg's friendship as one of the highest points of my motorcycle training life. It's in no small part because of the commitment to safety by folks like Greg that California has seen the first sustained reduction of motorcycle fatalities in our nation's history.

I truly hope that MotoJitsu and this book's contents continue to get riders everywhere to "Shut up and practice!"

Dave Bianco
Motorcycle Training Program Administrator/Manager
Camp Pendleton, CA

Preface

After publishing my first book, *MotoJitsu Master Riding Program*, I have been asked what other drills could help further develop necessary riding skills for the street. The drills outlined in this book are my answer.

With each drill I describe the dimensions, what gear to be in, recommended speeds, directions for it, techniques to practice, benefits each one will provide, and tips to help you succeed. Of course these are all recommendations; *you* will ultimately decide what's best for you in that moment depending on your skill and comfort. These drills could also be altered slightly to conform to the location you have available for practicing.

As you get comfortable, *slowly* attempt the drills at a faster pace. If you do, you may discover the level of precision you had at lower speeds starts to feel a bit sloppy after going faster. If this happens, refocus on the technique at a slower pace. Only with better technique will you be able to go faster without adding too much risk. Higher speeds without accurate technique will likely result in a crash and/or injury.

I started practicing these drills, or slight variations of them, soon after I began riding seven years ago. Sometimes I would spend hours working solely on one or two of them. Each drill is designed to give you specific challenges with enough flexibility to attempt at various speeds. For years I would practice alone but when I started inviting friends to do it with me, it became that much more effective and fun.

I sincerely hope you not only practice these drills consistently, but you do so with *joy in your heart* knowing that, performed correctly, these drills will enhance the likelihood of having the right technique when you need it the most.

To see demonstrations of each of the drills, search "MotoJitsu Master Riding Program Volume 2 Drills" on my YouTube channel, MotoJitsu (www.youtube.com/motojitsu).

Snowman

Gear: 1st or 2nd

Speed: 12–20 mph

Directions:

Part 1—Start just outside the 40 ft circle as pictured. Accelerate and turn left around the 20 ft circle and ride toward the 40 ft circle and turn left again. Repeat in an oval pattern. Practice going left until you are comfortable, then practice going right.

Part 2—Start just outside the 40 ft circle. Accelerate and ride in between the two circles as pictured. Turn right around the 20 ft circle first, then ride in between the circles again toward the 40 ft circle and turn left. Repeat in a figure 8 pattern. You may also start from the opposite side of the 40 ft circle to practice both left and right turns with various diameters.

Techniques to Practice: Vision, timing of your head turns, turn-in points, line selection, throttle control, and various braking techniques, including engine braking (solely rolling off the throttle to slow down) and trail braking (reducing brake pressure as the motorcycle leans into the turn) with the front brake only, rear only, and both at the same time to feel its effects.

Benefits: Overall confidence with turning, comfort leaning the motorcycle, and having an experiential understanding of how different diameter turns affect your technique, speed, and timing.

Tips: Turn your head and look toward the exit of each turn prior to leaning the bike. Your eyes should always be tracking to where you want to go next, not down at the front tire or cones on the ground. If you're practicing body position, the phrase "Body, Head, Bike" may help you with your sequence. Expect to drift too wide around the circles when first starting out; your target range is no more than 10 feet away from either circle.

Dimensions

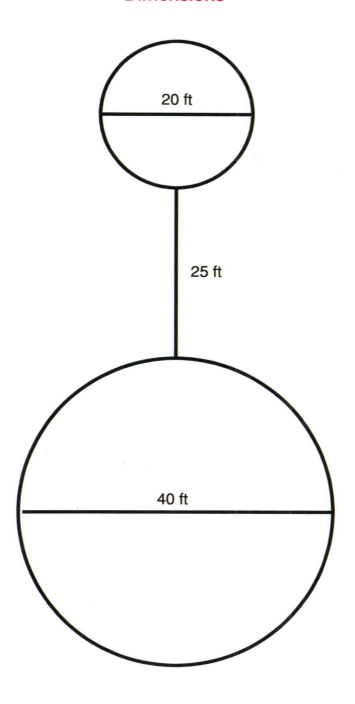

Part 1

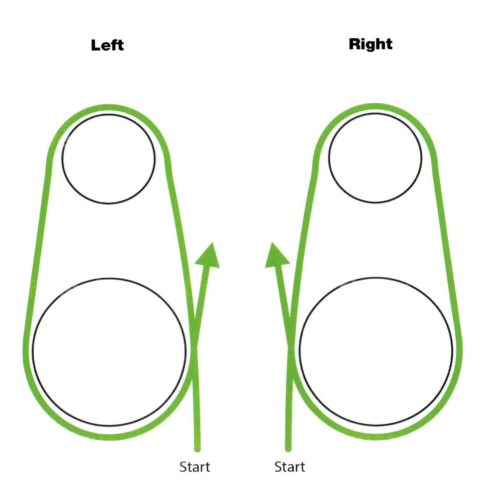

Part 2

Figure 8

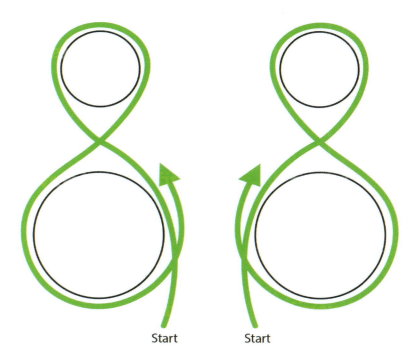

3 3s

Gear: 1st or 2nd

Speed: 10–20 mph

Directions:

Part 1—Start just outside the 30 ft circle as pictured. Ride straight and turn left around the 30 ft circle and ride toward the other 30 ft circle and turn left again. Repeat in an oval pattern. Practice going left until you are comfortable, then practice going right.

Part 2—Start just outside the 30 ft circle. Accelerate and ride in between the two circles as pictured. Turn right around the 30 ft circle first then ride toward the other 30 ft circle and turn left. Repeat in a figure 8 pattern.

Techniques to Practice: Head turns, body position, line selection, and transitioning from left to right turns back-to-back. Start by trying to maintain a near-constant speed for the entire drill, as if on cruise control. If you adjust your speed at all, do it solely with the throttle.

Benefits: Smooth throttle control, staying relaxed on the handlebars, cornering confidence with similar turns, and allowing yourself to feel what the bike is doing underneath you without adding additional inputs.

Tips: If you treat the throttle like an on/off switch, the bike will become jerky or unstable and will ultimately have less traction due to the throttle's effects on the suspension. Instead it may help to imagine the throttle as a dimmer switch using precise, fluid movements. Expect to not be able to maintain a near constant speed for the entire drill. The subtleness of your throttle inputs will directly correlate to your suspension, line, and confidence.

Dimensions

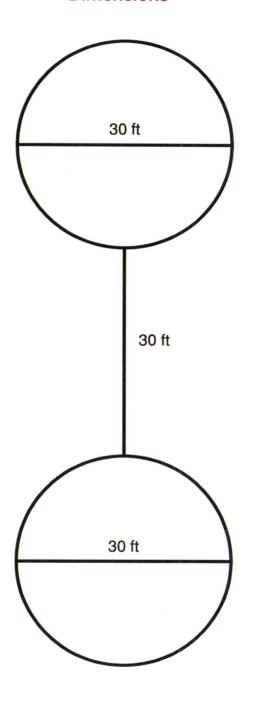

Part 1

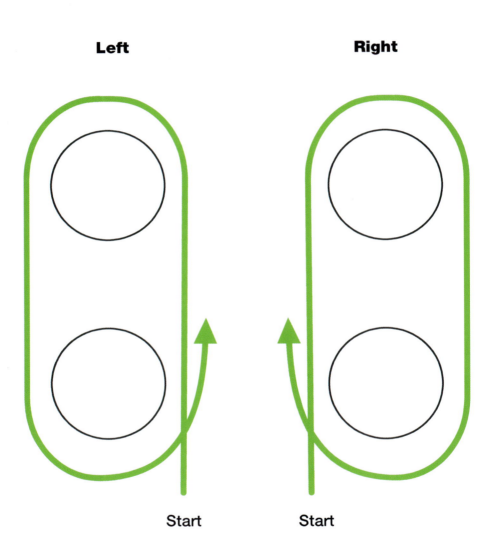

Part 2

Figure 8

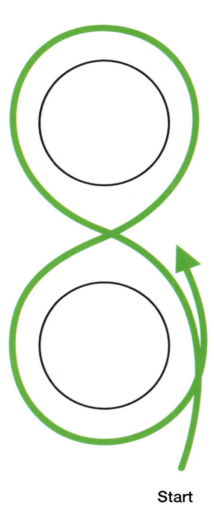

Start

Eyeballs

Gear: 1st

Speed: 8–15 mph

Directions:

Part 1—Start by riding inside the first 20 ft circle to the left as pictured. After one rotation, cross over into the other circle where they connect and ride in the opposite direction for one rotation before exiting.

Part 2—Start by riding inside the first 20 ft circle to the left as pictured. After two rotations, cross over into the other circle where they connect and ride in the opposite direction for two rotations before exiting.

Techniques to Practice: Vision, timing, body position, throttle control, clutch control, counter-balancing, rear brake usage, staying loose on the handlebars, and line selection.

Benefits: Confidence with your bike, reduction of anxiety while riding slowly, comfort making U-turns, and learning how much lean angle is required to complete tighter turns.

Tips: Turn your head and look at the opposite side of the circle from where you are. With larger head turns, the bike will naturally want to tighten its line. If you find yourself not able to make it and go wide, you may be going too slowly or may not be using all of the space available. If you ride through the same turn at a higher speed, the bike must lean more to complete it. For this drill, the bike must lean a great amount, therefore requiring you to ride faster than you think you should. If you have a low ground clearance bike, like a cruiser, your foot pegs or floorboards are likely to scrape the ground. If they do, try not to have a lot of weight pressing down on your foot; instead, shift more of your body weight to the opposite side of the bike (counter-balancing) so the foot peg or floorboard will skip across the ground easily.

If you're still going wide, ensure when you go into the circle, you're using all the space you have to complete the drill. Ride as close as you can to the line/cones to ensure you're not making the circles tighter than they need to be.

Dimensions

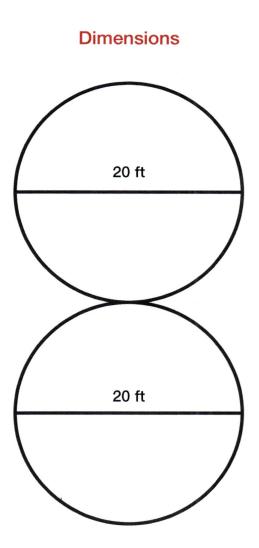

Part 1

Single

Part 2

Double

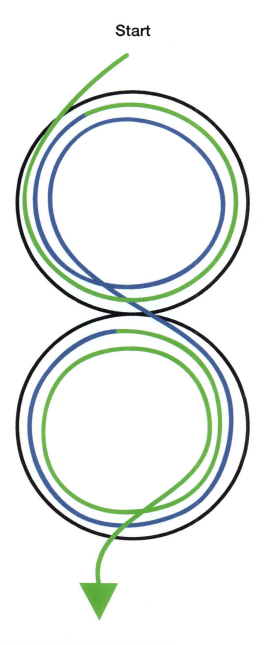

Don't Die

Gear: 2nd

Speed: 10–18 mph

Directions:

Part 1—Start at least 40 ft back from the entrance to the turn as pictured. Accelerate and upshift into 2nd gear prior to riding left into the turn. Once you're more than halfway through the turn, stop as quickly as you can without crossing the 10-foot line. Imagine the 10-foot line is a guardrail or a double yellow line. Practice going left until you are comfortable.

Part 2—Once you're comfortable going left, then practice going right.

Techniques to Practice: This drill focuses on stopping quickly in a curve, which requires a high level of focus and braking finesse. Practice with and without having your brakes covered to learn what gives you the best feel and the most confidence at various speeds. Start by braking near the halfway point until your technique improves. Ensure you're back in first gear before stopping to be ready to escape if needed.

Benefits: Confidence using the brakes in a turn, learning how to slow down and stop while leaned over, less anxiety going around a blind corner or riding on unfamiliar roads.

Tips: This requires an acute understanding of lean angle and brake pressure. The initial touch of the brakes should be very soft. If you add an abrupt input into the brakes while practicing this drill, you could lose all traction and crash. The goal is to add brake pressure as you bring the motorcycle upright, gaining traction. Start by only going 10 mph and slowly add speed when your technique improves. Expect yourself not to stop within the 10-foot limit line at first. That's OK. Practice until you can go into the turn at 18 mph and stop consistently without crossing over the 10-foot line.

Dimensions

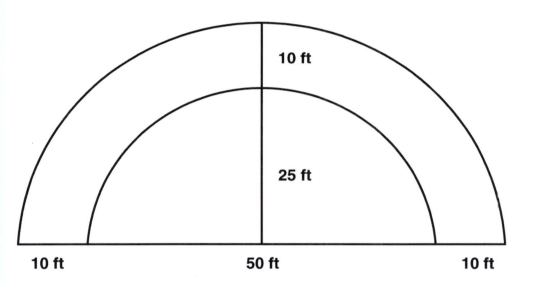

Part 1

Left

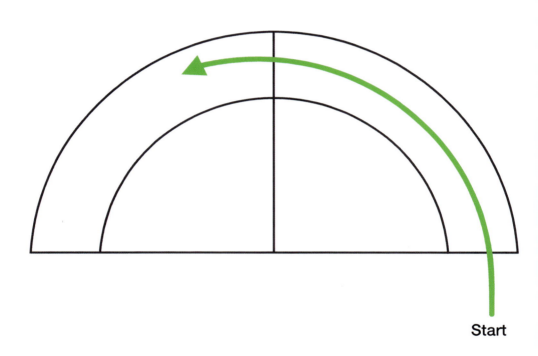

Start

Part 2

Right

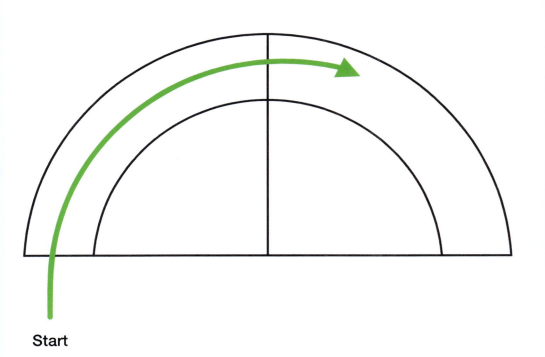

Start

Corner Speed

Gear: 1st or 2nd
Speed: 20–30 mph

Directions:

Part 1 — Start just outside the oval. Accelerate and ride toward the first turn, upshifting to 2nd gear. Turn left around the 40 ft circle and ride down the straightaway. Turn left again and repeat in an oval pattern. Slowly increase your speed on the straightaways while braking for the corners. Practice going left until you are comfortable.

Part 2 — Once you're comfortable going left, then practice going right.

Techniques to Practice: Vision, head turns, turn-in points, acceleration out of the corners, line selection, body position, and throttle control. This drill is meant for higher speed turns — around 30 mph on the straights and slowing down to no less than 20 mph for the corners is ideal. Your goal is to not run wide at the exit — stay within 10-foot of the cones.

Benefits: Turning confidence at faster speeds with repeating turns, comfort leaning the motorcycle, braking certainty, and line selection. This drill is great to practice full body position due to its higher speed. If desired, try knee down. This drill will also provide an experiential understanding of the level of grip your tires are providing with your current location.

Tips: Turn your head and look toward the opposite side of each turn prior to leaning the bike. Your eyes should be tracking where you want to end up, looking far ahead while managing your line with your peripheral vision. If you're practicing full body position, having your body stay in place for the drill, even on the straightaways, may build comfort with the position and how it affects the bike's ability to turn. Expect to go wide at the exits at first. A few causes are having too quick of an entry speed for your skill, turning in too early, not steering the bike quickly enough, not looking where you want to go, and not countersteering effectively.

Dimensions

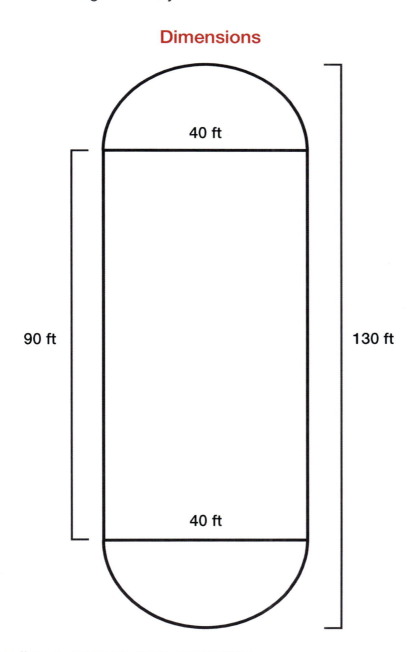

Part 1

Left

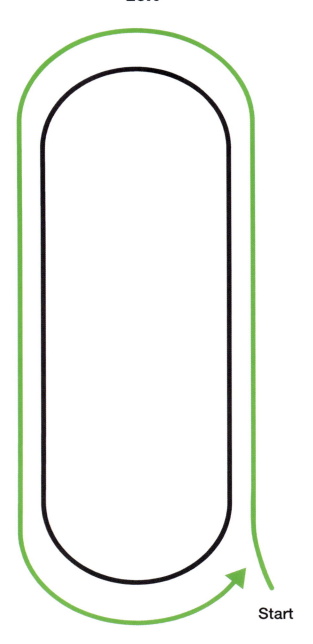

Part 2

Right

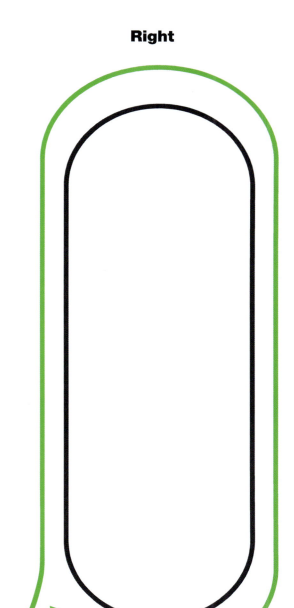

Start

Crazy 13

Gear: 1st

Speed: 5–15 mph

Directions:

Part 1—Begin at the start line as pictured. Accelerate and ride to the left of the first cone, right of the second, then another left around the third cone. Ride in between the cones at the opposite end and make a left U-turn. Repeat the cone weave on the opposite side.

Part 2—Continue riding and make a right U-turn around the first cone. Make a left U-turn around the middle cone on the opposite side of the drill. Continue to make another right U-turn around the last cone. Repeat the weave going back to the finish line as pictured.

This timed drill starts when your front tire crosses the start line and stops when your front tire crosses the finish line.

- **Beginner: 40–60 seconds**
- **Intermediate: 30–40 seconds**
- **Advanced: 25–30 seconds**
- **Expert: 25 seconds or less**

Techniques to Practice: Vision, timing, body position, throttle control, clutch control, counter-balancing, trail braking, quick steering, line selection, countersteering.

Benefits: This drill sharpens the most important aspect of street riding—your judgment. You'll make quick decisions, plan ahead, look where you want to go, complete multiple U-turns in a row, and challenge yourself against the clock.

Tips: Vision is the key factor for success. If you're not looking ahead and planning your line, even just completing the drill will be challenging.

Dimensions

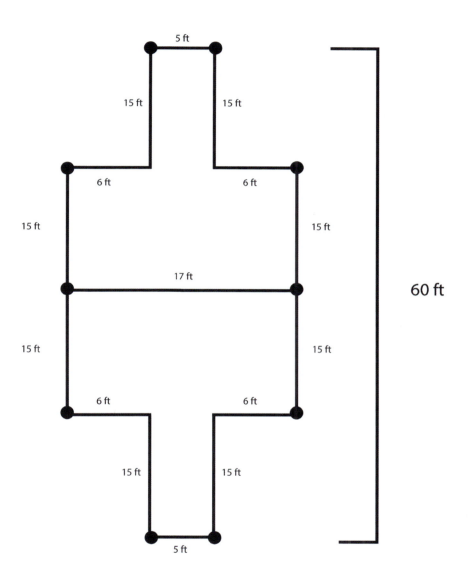

- Small cone or tennis ball cut in half

Part 1

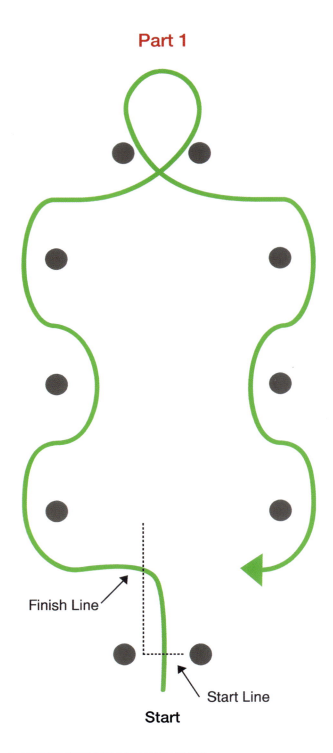

Part 2

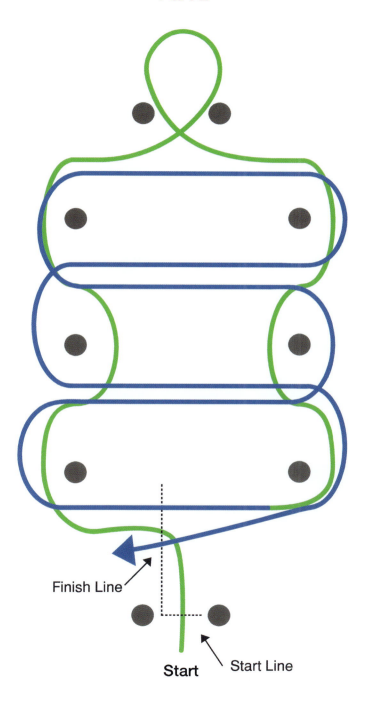

Conversion to Metric

The need for safety is universal; systems of measurement are not. The chart below converts measurements used in the drills so you can practice and master them anywhere you may be.

Drill	Measurement	US	Global
Snowman	Distance	20, 25, 40 ft	6.0, 7.6, 12.1 m
Snowman	Speed	12-20 MPH	19-32 KPH
3 3s	Distance	30 ft	9.1 m
3 3s	Speed	10-20 MPH	16-32 KPH
Eyeballs	Distance	20 ft	6 m
Eyeballs	Speed	8-15 MPH	13-24 KPH
Don't Die	Distance	10, 25, 50 ft	3.0, 7.6, 15.2 m
Don't Die	Speed	10-18 MPH	16-29 KPH
Corner Speed	Distance	40, 90, 130 ft	12.1, 27.4, 39.6 m
Corner Speed	Speed	20-30 MPH	32-48 KPH
Crazy 13	Distance	5, 6, 15, 17, 60 ft	1.5, 1.8, 4.6, 5.1, 18.2 m
Crazy 13	Speed	5-15 MPH	8-24 KPH

What's the Point?

For the past seven years, I have been practicing in various parking lots, motorcycle training areas, and local tracks to deepen my understanding and abilities on the motorcycle. The first time you have to do an emergency stop mid-corner shouldn't be on the public roads. A rider who doesn't practice is like a person who can't swim jumping directly into the deep end of a pool, hoping they can float. Hope is not a technique to rely upon.

All the drills in this book and inside *MotoJitsu Master Riding Program* answer the question what to practice. Practicing sharpens the techniques you have learned. Formal training, books, and videos can give you the tools in your tool belt, but they still may be wrapped in plastic or inside cardboard boxes.

If you were to attempt surgery with a butter knife, expect the job to be horribly executed. You'll need a tremendous amount of energy and it isn't going to look very good. Now imagine you have a scalpel. Your incision will be precise, little effort will be needed, and you may not even leave a scar. Practice sharpens your tools.

Your goal isn't to be the rider with only a few tools around your waist but rather the rider with an entire hardware store as your toolbox. Having access to the right tool when you need it is crucial for street riding. You may not need every tool for every ride or every corner, but at least you'll know which tool is needed moment-to-moment.

Be prepared in case it starts raining and the traction drops, a car does a U-turn in front of you, or a group ride leads you to an unfamiliar road with downhill, decreasing radius blind corners you weren't expecting.

Do not rely upon chance. Trust the techniques you have learned through formal training and the wisdom you have gained by practicing.

Lastly, practicing is incredibly fun to do. Even if there wasn't a reason to practice nor did it provide any advantage in your skills, I still would multiple times a week. There doesn't have to be a reason to watch a sunset or listen to music—the act itself is the point.

Printed in Great Britain
by Amazon